lace

READING
A Pictorial History

Christchurch, on Whitley Hill, has been a Reading landmark for over a century. In 1862, when it was first built, it stood in the middle of fields. It was built to accommodate the overspill from St Giles', as the population in this part of Reading grew.

READING

A Pictorial History

Stuart Hylton

Phillimore

1994

Published by
PHILLIMORE & CO. LTD.
Shopwyke Manor Barn, Chichester, Sussex

ISBN 0 85033 919 7

Printed and bound in Great Britain by
BIDDLES LTD.
Guildford, Surrey

To my parents

List of Illustrations

Frontispiece: Christchurch, *c.*1862

Acknowledgements

The heart of this selection of pictures comes from the local history library's collection at Central Library in Kings Road. No matter how busy they were, Margaret Smith and her colleagues have always been enormously helpful to me in preparing this book.

Reading Newspapers very kindly allowed me to draw on their archives (now held by the Museum of Reading) for many of my pictures of Reading in the 1930s and 1940s.

Staff at the Museum of Reading were most helpful to me, in allowing access to their collection and in other ways. Particular thanks go to Sue Read and Godfrey Omer-Parsons.

A number of private collectors were kind enough to allow me to use illustrations from their collections. I am especially grateful to Graham Parlour, John Griffin and Mary Kift.

Richard Reed of photographers White and Reed did an expert job in reproducing (and often, it seemed, improving upon) many of the original photographs.

The Trustees of the Science Museum allowed me to reproduce from their collection the early photographs of Reading by Fox-Talbot.

Michael Bott, archivist at the University of Reading, helped me with the section on the university and its predecessors.

Janet Tait provided the illustrations for the endpapers of the book.

Friends, colleagues, acquaintances and complete strangers made comments and suggestions and provided information which has added greatly to my knowledge of the history of Reading, even if there was not space for it all to find its way into the book.

Any errors or omissions remaining in the book, despite all this good advice, are entirely my own responsibility.

Once again, my wife and children bore with great fortitude the suffering and neglect resulting from my writing a book.

Introduction

Reading is often held up as being the average British town; market researchers use it as a barometer of public opinion for that reason. In much the same way, the history of the town reflects that of the nation. For more than a thousand years, Reading has been host to many of the people and events that have helped to shape modern Britain.

Parliaments have met here, royalty were married and buried in the abbey. The men of Reading went off to fight in the battle of Agincourt and the town's workshops made the sailcloth that carried part of Nelson's fleet to Trafalgar. The battles of the Civil War and the so-called 'bloodless' revolution of 1688 were fought out in its streets and the fields around. There have also been less violent revolutions—in transport, with the coming of the canal and the railways, and the Industrial Revolution itself, when the town's major manufacturers made the name of Reading known throughout the world.

The town was founded in about the seventh century, by a man called Reada ('the red') and his followers, the Readingas. They built it near to where the River Kennet joins the Thames and the waterways have been important to Reading on many occasions in its history. In the earliest days, they carried invading Danes who destroyed the town during a raid in the year 1006. It is likely that the settlement was at that time centred around the area now occupied by St Mary's Butts.

The destruction may have included one of Reading's earliest places of worship. Queen Elfrida, mother of Ethelred the Unready, is said to have built a nunnery on the site of St Mary's church. She did so in atonement for having the 15-year-old King Edward of the West Saxons—her own stepson—murdered at Corfe Castle in A.D.978. No trace of the original nunnery now remains; it is thought to have been destroyed by marauding Danes during one of their raids up the Thames. However, parts of the present church are thought to date back as far as the early 13th century or earlier.

By the time of Domesday Book, Reading was one of only two places in Berkshire important enough to be listed as a borough (Wallingford was the other). It was recorded as belonging to the king and included two agricultural estates, four mills operating on the River Kennet and at least one on the Thames, at Caversham.

William the Conqueror ceded land in Reading to the abbey at Battle, near Hastings, scene of his victory over King Harold. This part of Reading is known to the present day as Battle. It was his youngest son, Henry I, who founded Reading's own abbey, following the drowning of his son on his way home from Normandy in 1120. Henry I was himself to be buried in the part-completed abbey in 1135, his body having been brought back from France, sewn in a bull's hide.

The scale of the abbey was breathtaking. Its centrepiece was the Great Church, which was the size of Westminster Abbey or Durham Cathedral. The church was consecrated by Thomas à Becket in 1164, in the presence of Henry II. For 400 years, the abbey dominated the life of the town and made Reading one of the most important religious and political centres in the country. Parliament used to meet there whenever outbreaks of the plague drove them out of London, and it became one of the richest monasteries in the land. The abbot was made lord of the manor of Reading and had rights to dispense justice, control trade and generally regulate the life of the town. This led to longstanding grievances between town and abbey which occasionally erupted into violence on the streets. As a result, a case was brought to the king's court in the year 1253 and, later that same year, led to the granting of the town's first charter.

This gave the townspeople some degree of independence from the abbey and was to regulate relations between the two until the abbey's dissolution. The town developed rapidly in the Middle Ages as a market and a manufacturing centre. Woollen cloth and leather goods were among Reading's most important products during this period.

The influence of the abbey also caused the centre of gravity of the town to shift, away from St Mary's Butts towards Market Place. For many centuries after, the area around Market Place was the focal point for trade and for the celebration of important events in the life of the town.

Some authorities also believe that the foundation of Reading School coincides with that of the abbey, making Reading School the tenth oldest in the country. Certainly, the first abbot was given the authority to carry out secular duties, such as teaching, in addition to his religious responsibilities.

In the year 1216, Henry III succeeded to the throne at the age of nine. For the next two years, the country was effectively governed by William, the Earl Marshal of England, who lived at the estate at Caversham Park. William, who had been instrumental in getting King John to sign the Magna Carta, was by this time in his eighties. When he returned to Caversham Park to spend the final days of his life there, the whole of the royal household came with him from London.

The town's other major religious community—the Franciscan Grey Friars, who gave their name to Friar Street—came to Reading in 1234. Thanks to a letter from the pope, they persuaded the Abbot of Reading to give them a piece of land near Caversham Bridge to set up their community. This swampy site proved to be unsuitable for their needs and, helped by the intervention of the Archbishop of Canterbury, they secured the site at the end of Friar Street where Greyfriars church stands to this day.

The dominance of the Abbey was to end in 1539, when Henry VIII dissolved the monasteries. The last abbot, Hugh Cook Faringdon (later canonised) was hung, drawn and quartered in the streets of Reading and the long process of the abbey's destruction began. For centuries, it became a useful source of building materials. Stone and timber from it found their way into many Reading buildings, including St Mary's church. Other materials were shipped downstream, to London or to help with construction at Windsor Castle. Virtually all that remains today are the flint inner walls of the Chapter House, the Abbey Gateway and part of the Hospitium (the latter two having undergone much restoration in the 19th century).

Greyfriars church also went into a long period of decline following the dissolution. This culminated in the roofless shell being used as the town's gaol. It was eventually restored in 1863 and stands today as the most complete surviving example of Franciscan architecture in the country.

It was shortly after the dissolution that Julius Palmer, who had previously been the master of Reading School, also suffered the fate of a martyr. He saw the Protestants

Latimer and Ridley die during the reign of Mary Tudor and was inspired by it to write a pamphlet in opposition. This was seized upon by his enemies and ended in his being burnt at the stake in Newbury in 1555.

Queen Elizabeth I was to take a great interest in the affairs of the town. She was a regular visitor, having her own private pew in St Laurence's church. In 1560, she granted the town one of its most important charters, greatly extending its powers of self-government. By this time, the original guildhall (which stood in the area known today as Yield Hall) had been abandoned and the affairs of the borough were administered, first from the former Greyfriars church and later from the upper floor of the old abbey hospitium (the lower floor of which was by now occupied by Reading School). Elizabeth I also encouraged local industries, including silk making, which was to become important to the town during the 17th and 18th centuries.

Several other benefactors also left their mark on the town around this time. Sir Thomas White was a Reading-born clothier who went on to found St John's College, Oxford. Reading School was endowed with scholarships to the college. John Kendrick also made his fortune in the clothing trade. In 1624 he left a bequest that was used to construct the Oracle, a workhouse to give the poor of Reading employment in the clothing industry. In the event, the charity was badly administered over the years, though it did help pay for the founding of Kendrick School in 1877. John Blagrave was a member of a wealthy local landowning family and the leading mathematician of his time. His charitable works included improvements to Market Place and the construction of the Blagrave Piazza, which stood on the south side of St Laurence's church. The church still contains a monument to Blagrave, though the piazza itself (see plate 7) was demolished in the mid-19th century.

It was also during Queen Elizabeth's reign that William Laud was born in Reading. The son of a clothier, he was born in a house which stood roughly where Queen Victoria Street now joins Broad Street. He was later to become the widely unpopular Archbishop of Canterbury and henchman of King Charles I, and was executed by Parliament in 1645. Despite his close involvement in the politics of the nation in the years leading up to the Civil War, he retained a close interest in the affairs of the borough throughout his life and, in fact, did much good for Reading.

The Civil War itself, however, did nothing but harm to the town. Reading was heavily fortified by the Royalists (the abbey again providing some of the materials for the fortifications) and the Parliamentary forces laid siege to it. It was only captured after a prolonged (and for the town damaging) struggle, in which King Charles himself intervened at one point in an attempt to gain control of Caversham Bridge. Thereafter, the town had troops from one side or the other visited upon it for the duration of the Civil War. The demands of the various garrisons (which extended at one point to kidnapping and ransoming the mayor to raise funds) left Reading impoverished for many years afterwards.

A further unwelcome visitation of troops was sent to the town by King James I, after the landing of William of Orange at Torbay in 1688. The townspeople were convinced that these Irish Catholic forces were planning to steal their valuables and murder them in their beds. They sent for help from William's advancing forces and a running battle ensued in the streets of Reading. James' troops were driven out of Reading with a loss of 53 killed or wounded. They were just about the only casualties of the revolution.

The 17th century was also marked by a number of serious outbreaks of the plague in Reading, brought about by a total ignorance of the most basic tenets of public health.

The causes of the plague were not understood at this time and the only remedy open to the townspeople was to isolate victims in a property called the pest house, in Conduit Close, off Whitley Street.

In addition to their military significance, the waterways soon became important to the town as a trade route. As early as 1404, the abbey and the Merchants' Guild were charging tolls for the passage of boats along the Kennet. The importance of the waterways grew dramatically in 1715 with the passage of the Kennet Navigation Act and the start of works to make the Kennet navigable as far as Newbury.

The townspeople were worried that this would result in the town losing trade. A rioting mob of local people (led by one-time mayor Robert Blake, who later gave his name to Blake's Lock) tried to destroy the navigation works and there were also threats against the lives of the bargees who traded along the canal. Their efforts came to nothing and the Kennet Navigation opened to traffic in 1723. In fact, their fears proved to be unfounded and the town prospered from being on the canal. This was particularly the case after 1810, when the Kennet and Avon Canal connected London and Bristol via Reading and barges of up to 200 tons and 110 ft. in length were making their way through the town.

Transport of one kind or another has been important in much of Reading's growth. The town became an important stopping off point for stage coaches travelling between London and the spa at Bath, made popular by Queen Anne. Some of the coaching inns built to cater for that passing trade—such as the *Sun* and the *George*—exist to this day.

However, the days of both the coaches and the canal were numbered from 1835, when Parliamentary approval was given for the construction of the Great Western Railway from London to Bristol. Brunel's broad gauge railway reached Maidenhead by 1838 and Reading itself entered the railway age in 1840. It was joined in 1849 by the London and South Eastern Railway, which linked Reading to Waterloo.

The railways soon gave Reading trading links with the rest of the nation and beyond, and were important in the development of the town's famous 'three Bs'—beer, biscuits and bulbs. These three major employers had much to do with the town's growth and prosperity in the 19th century.

William Simonds established his brewery in Broad Street in 1785. Part of his early success was founded on supplying beer to the British army. The business expanded rapidly and he was soon able to move to larger premises on Bridge Street, which eventually became a huge brewery complex that continued in operation until 1980. Simonds also diversified into banking and in 1836 commissioned the ornate bank building on King Street, now occupied by Barclays Bank but which still bears his name on the door.

The Huntley and Palmer's story began with Hannah Huntley, the wife of an Oxfordshire schoolteacher, selling biscuits to stagecoach travellers passing by the school gate. Her stepson, Joseph, moved to Reading in 1811 and subsequently set up a biscuit-making business in London Street. One of their great breakthroughs was the use of decorated tinplate boxes to keep the biscuits fresh, an idea which stemmed from Huntley's son working for a nearby ironmonger. George Palmer joined the partnership in 1841 and the business grew until, at its height, it employed 6,000 people.

Huntley and Palmer's biscuits were sold all over the world, often reaching areas otherwise untouched by western civilisation. Explorers in the jungles of New Guinea found a headhunter wearing a Huntley and Palmer's biscuit tin lid around his neck on a cord, like a medal, and Huntley and Palmer's biscuits were found in the Dalai Lama's palace by the first Westerners to enter it.

John Sutton set up his corn and seed merchant's business in Reading in 1807. It was the business acumen of his son, Martin Hope Sutton, that developed it into a national business. Their success was based upon a reputation for honesty and reliability, in a business which was not at the time noted for these qualities. Their advice was sought by the Government during the Irish Potato Famine of 1845. By the 1920s their business had expanded to cover much of the area between Market Place, The Forbury, Abbey Street and Kings Road. The Sutton family were active in the life of the town, one of their number helping in 1893 to establish the University Extension College which was later to become Reading University.

These major employers were one of the reasons for the town's rapid growth during the 19th century. Reading's population increased from less than 10,000 in 1801 to over 72,000 (on expanded boundaries) by the beginning of the 20th century. It was during this period that many of the services and institutions that Reading people take for granted today were established.

Reading had a deserved reputation for being a very unhealthy place to live at the beginning of the 19th century. One of the reasons for this was the water supply. Much of it was drawn from the Kennet that also served as a public sewer. It was pumped along pipes made from bored-out elm trees and stored in a lead reservoir which stood in the centre of Broad Street. In the 1820s a water tower was erected to supply some of the higher houses, but there was still no proper system of purification. It was 1850 before the town's waterworks was built at Fobney, upstream of where the pollution of Reading poured into the Kennet. Even so, the inadequacies of the water supply meant that, at least until 1874, supplies of water had to be turned off at night.

Improvements to this and other public utilities were hampered by the existence of a strong lobby of 'economisers' on the council. These people advanced some extraordinary arguments against any kind of public investment—for example, that it was 'impious' to try to thwart God's will by preventing disease, and that the provision of a hospital in Reading would only attract sick and delicate people to the town. Thus it was not until 1867 that the council acquired land at Manor Farm on which to build a proper sewage works and serious efforts to improve the town's sanitation could begin. Subsequent extensions of Reading's boundaries resulted in part from the desire of the people living in neighbouring communities to be connected to Reading's sewerage system.

Health care had an equally difficult time getting established in Reading. In 1802, the People's Dispensary was founded in the town, providing a very basic medical service for the ordinary people. By the 1870s, one in three of Reading's population subscribed to it.

The establishment of the Royal Berkshire Hospital owes much to the persistence of a retired bank clerk called Richard Oliver. He lobbied a wide range of people in his efforts to provide the town with proper health care. They include King William IV (whose royal patronage is reflected in the hospital's name), Lord Sidmouth (who, as Henry Addington, was the only prime minister to come from Reading, and who donated the land on which it was built) and the Great Western Railway (which provided both part of the building costs and many of the initial patients during the hazardous construction of the London to Bristol railway). The hospital was opened in 1839 and its original building, fronting onto London Road, can still be seen. The need for a hospital was illustrated by the fact that it had doubled in size by 1866. It was perhaps fitting that Richard Oliver should end his days in the hospital, after being knocked down by a horse-drawn wagon in London Street.

The 19th century also saw some major developments in transport in Reading. In addition to the railways, 1877 saw the construction of the first horse-drawn tramway, between Cemetery Junction and Brock Barracks on the Oxford road. The private company which ran it was bought out by the council in 1901 who immediately introduced plans to electrify it and to extend the network of routes.

Many other public services came into being during this period. The Watch Committee acquired two fire engines in 1844, but a separate fire brigade was only established in 1862. Even after this, the vagaries of the water supply referred to earlier made their job a very difficult one. It was a serious fire at the Great Western Railway works in 1874, which went out of control due to water shortages, that led to the construction of a new reservoir at Bath Road. In addition to the public fire service, several major local manufacturers, insurance companies and even some private individuals (such as the Crawshay family of Caversham Park) had their own fire brigades.

The University of Reading is, strictly speaking, a 20th-century creation (it received its charter in 1926). However, its origins lay in the 19th century, in classes run in the Art School in West Street and the Science School, based in the old Reading School buildings (where the museum now stands). They combined to form the Reading University Extension College, opened under the auspices of Christ Church, Oxford in 1892. It moved from its original home in Valpy Street to new premises in London Road in 1906, where it remained until the university acquired the Whiteknights estate as its campus in 1947.

Reading School entered a period of decline after the long stewardship of its most famous headmaster, Dr. Valpy, ended in 1830. A new system of management for the school was brought in by Act of Parliament in 1867, giving greater powers to the local authority. A new site was acquired and architect Alfred Waterhouse was brought in to design the present school buildings. This period of the school's history also saw much debate as to whether its role was to serve purely local needs, or those of a fee-paying élite. The matter was resolved in 1908 when Reading School came fully under local authority control.

The administrative boundaries of the borough were expanded in 1877 and 1911 to reflect the growth of the built-up area. The first extension brought in Newtown, developed largely to house the growing numbers of Huntley and Palmer's employees. In 1911 the extension brought parts of Tilehurst and most of Caversham into the borough. The only part of Caversham not to be incorporated into Reading at that time was the estate of Caversham Park, on the grounds that the estate would never be developed! As a condition of the latter extension, a wider Caversham bridge had to be provided (though this was not completed until 1926). Prior to this, the new Reading Bridge was opened in 1923 to handle the growing traffic crossing the river.

In the 20th century, the growth of the town has continued and the built-up area has once again spread well beyond the present administrative boundaries.

Reading was affected by the two world wars in all sorts of ways, but was largely spared the widespread destruction from bombing suffered by some other towns and cities. The one serious bombing raid, in 1943, was on the eastern end of Friar Street (including the Town Hall and St Laurence's church) and left almost a hundred people dead or seriously injured.

Recent years have seen the town change from one known principally for its manufacturing industries to a largely service-based economy. Simond's Bridge Street brewery, by now part of the Courage brewing empire, was relocated in 1980 to Worton Grange, a new 70-acre site beside the motorway to the south of the town. Suttons Seeds moved their business to Torquay in 1974 and their trial grounds were later to become the Suttons Industrial Park. Huntley and Palmer's biscuit manufacture continued in the town until 1977 and their administrative offices in the town closed in the 1980s. A lasting reminder of the firm's impact on Reading is the park bearing George Palmer's name, which he donated to the town.

The electric trams, whose introduction caused so much excitement in 1903, were replaced by trolley buses in 1939 and these in turn gave way to the motor bus after the war. High Speed Trains, taking full advantage of Brunel's superb railway engineering skills, cut journey times to London to 24 minutes.

But the main transport story since the war has been one of Reading's attempts to come to terms with the private car. The coming of the M4 to the town in 1971 added to its attractions as a headquarters for office-based companies and computer industries. The congestion caused by traffic within the town worked in precisely the opposite direction. On the one hand, we have seen the attempts to accommodate the car (such as the Inner Distribution Road, which for so long ended in an unfinished 'ski jump'). On the other, there have been moves to tame the car, such as the recent pedestrianisation of the town centre. Often in Reading's history, the town's fortunes have turned upon transport issues. How Reading manages to cope with the car may well hold the key to the town's future prosperity.

Despite all the change that has taken place, there is still much evidence to be seen of Reading's past. The town has over 800 listed historic buildings and even many of the place names and street names have connections with the people and events that have shaped the history of the town.

In particular, there is a rich legacy of pictorial history, dating back to the very birth of the camera and beyond. The founding father of modern photography, W.H. Fox-Talbot, chose the town as the base for his fledgling business. As a result, Reading has one of the earliest photographic records of any town in the world.

No less valuable are the works of the many photographers—often unknown—who have captured the slices of Reading life over the last 150 years that are contained in this book. I have tried to include scenes that will be familiar to those who know the town today, others that have changed out of all recognition, the great celebrations and disasters that have occurred in the recent history of the town, as well as previous generations of Readingensians going about their daily lives.

Reading Before the Camera

1 Reading, as seen from the top of St Peter's church in 1750. A photograph from the same viewpoint about a century later can be seen elsewhere in the book (plate 26). At this time, the churches were the dominant architectural features of the town.

2 Reading seen from Whitley Hill to the south. It was drawn by Henry Burn in 1847, just as Fox-Talbot was taking the first photographic images of the town. By this time Huntley and Palmer's factory, the railway and the water tower can all be seen. The picture is dedicated to Mary Russell Mitford, a Reading resident who achieved fame as an author in the early 19th century.

3 St Laurence's church, seen from The Forbury. The presence of the old town hall dates the picture as after 1786. The open area was the subject of a dispute between the townspeople and Reading School, which was resolved by the townspeople occupying it with a protest cricket match.

4 The village of Caversham, as it would have looked from the Great Western Railway station, in about 1840 when the railway reached Reading.

5 The first of four of W.H. Timms' 'Select views of the borough of Reading', published in 1823. This one is looking westwards along King Street. In the distance can be seen the row of properties that until 1862 stood in the centre of Broad Street.

6 The view southwards up what is now Southampton Street (and was then called Horne Street) in 1823. St Giles' church has not yet been restored. A photograph taken from almost the same position in 1887 can be seen in the section on inns (see plate 80).

7 Market Place, 1823. St Laurence's church still has the Blagrave Piazza, built with a bequest from John Blagrave. Among other things, it housed the town's pillory, tumbril and ducking stool. It was said to have been the site of much vice and depravity, which may help to account for its demolition in 1869.

8 Duke Street, seen from the High Bridge in 1823. On the left-hand side of the bridge is the nightwatchman's sentrybox. These reluctant defenders of the peace protected the town until the establishment of the Borough Police Force in 1836.

9 Reading's two stations, in the early days of rail travel. The presence of the South Eastern Railway station dates the picture at some time after 1849. In those days, the station afforded a clear view across the river and to Caversham.

Earliest Images: Fox-Talbot

10   William Henry Fox-Talbot, founding father of modern photography, set up his business at 55 Baker Street (then called Russell Terrace) in the winter of 1843/4. This scene of London Street includes Lovejoy's bookshop and the newly-erected Mechanics' Institute (which later became a Primitive Methodist chapel and a theatre).

11 This picture of St Mary's church shows how it looked before its restoration in the 1860s. Fox-Talbot was never warmly received in Reading. His habit of working in the dark and using copious amounts of paper earned him an unenviable reputation as a banknote forger! His employment of 'a foreigner'—Dutchman, Nicholas Henneman—to manage his business was also regarded as suspect.

12 The Oracle was a workhouse, completed in 1628, and funded by a bequest from John Kendrick, a wealthy Reading-born clothier. It stood on the south side of Gun Street, on land later occupied by the brewery. This photograph shows the imposing gateway, just before its demolition in 1850.

13 Some of these Elizabethan buildings in Castle Street survive little changed to the present day. The building on the right is an early 18th-century addition. Fox-Talbot moved his business to London in 1847, but left behind what may be a uniquely early record of a provincial English town.

14 St Giles' church in Southampton Street suffered severe damage during the Civil War siege of 1643. It was founded as long ago as 1191, and this photograph shows it as it was before its 'restoration' by Victorian architect J.P. St. Aubyn in 1871-3.

15 The Abbey gateway in 1845. What we see today is largely a Victorian restoration by eminent architect Giles Gilbert Scott, after the building collapsed in the storms of 1861. The signs of structural failure can be seen in this photograph. Jane Austen spent part of her schooldays here.

Lost Landmarks

16   This photograph shows Finch's Buildings, a piece of ancient Reading. They survived in Hosier Street (near where the market now stands) until at least 1957, when this photograph was taken. Once the home of the Vachells, one of Reading's noble families, they were originally built in the 16th century. Some of the building materials in them may have come from Reading Abbey at the time of its dissolution. They were converted into a row of cottages in the 18th century.

17 Some old houses which were actually built into the walls of Reading Abbey. These may be the properties known as Abbey Wall, whose construction was promoted by Queen Elizabeth I when she visited the town in 1568. They were photographed in 1925, about two years before their demolition.

18 The *Griffin Inn* on Church Road, Caversham during its demolition in 1905. The landlord of the *Griffin* used to have the rights to the eel traps, or bucks, which stood in the Thames to the rear of the inn (shown in a later picture). These gave their name to a nearby lane, Buckside.

19 Caversham Priory used to stand at the junction of Church Street and Hemdean Road. The Worthington family, who lived there in about 1860, are in the centre of this photograph. On the left is Mr. Banks, the gardener, and on the right is the Rev. Joshua Bennett, the Rector of Caversham.

20 The Green School in Broad Street, photographed in about 1875. It was founded in 1782 by local aldermen and clergy to train up girls for a life as apprentices or domestic servants. It moved from St Mary's Butts to Broad Street in 1790, where it remained until the 1880s.

21 From 1603 or earlier, until Reading Bridge opened in 1923, a ramshackle footbridge called 'the Clappers' provided the only way across the Thames at the eastern end of the town. It was from here that Victorian murderess Annie Dyer threw a series of infant victims into the river. This photograph dates from about 1890, just before the murders took place.

22 Holmes furniture store in St Mary's Butts, shortly before its demolition and rebuilding in 1932 to create space for road widening.

23 The broad expanse of St Mary's Butts was once filled by buildings in its centre and along its eastern side, in front of the churchyard. This photograph dates from 1886, shortly before the buildings' demolition.

Caversham Mill

24 The mill at Caversham dates back to the days of Edward the Confessor, when it was held by a Saxon lord called Suain. It was still in use around 1910. Today, its only remains are the mill pond at Mill Road, at the end of Gosbrook Road. This photograph dates from around 1911.

25 Southcote Manor was a moated manor house, which had been acquired by the Blagrave family in the 16th century. A house had stood on the site since the 13th century. The estate remained in the family until the 1920s, but had been allowed to decay over many years. The picture was taken in 1921, immediately before the demolition of the house.

Seen from Above

26 The view from the tower of St Peter's church, Caversham, looking towards Reading. It is before 1869, because the old 'half and half' bridge is still in place. Reading remains a distant prospect, far away across the fields. The building in the foreground is Caversham Court, from 1799 the home of the Simonds brewing family. The house was built for them in the 1840s by Augustus Pugin, on the site of a much older building.

27 *(above)* St Mary's Butts, *c.*1930. The Simonds brewery can be seen to the right and the trams are working their way along Broad Street, which also has a taxi rank in the middle. The People's Dispensary in Chain Street is just visible to the left of the church.

28 *(above right)* A view of the station area, taken in about 1922. It shows the extent of the land then occupied by the railway. The old post office is under construction on the former site of the *Queen's Hotel*. Part of the area east of Market Place, occupied by Suttons Seeds, can be seen. The old South Eastern Railway station is centre right and part of the future site of the Apex Plaza office building is used for allotments.

29 *(below right)* An aerial view of the Huntley and Palmer factory, *c.*1920, showing something of the extent of their premises. Their network of private railway sidings can also be seen. Reading prison, in its pre-modernisation 'castle' form, is towards the top of the picture.

30 The town centre seen from the west in 1922. The triangular area of open space (called 'the triangle') is roughly on the site of the Chatham Street roundabout. The vacant site next to it will eventually be occupied by the Cooperative department store. McIlroys store dominates the Oxford Road and, on the right, is the area of housing and small business that will eventually be swallowed up by the Broad Street Mall.

31 Looking down along Chain Street from the north side of Broad Street in 1923. Silver's, the men's outfitters, had by now replaced Poynder's bookshop on the corner. Chain Street is so called because a chain was installed across Minster Street at its junction with Chain Street, to control vehicular access in the 17th century.

Reading Street Scenes

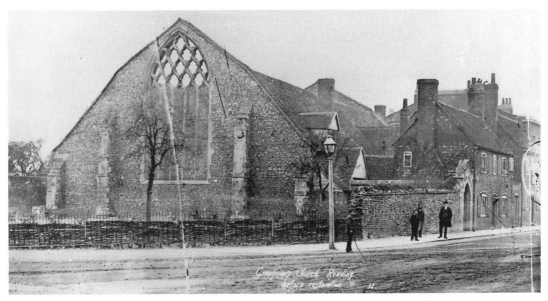

32 Greyfriars church, a roofless ruin prior to its restoration in 1863. Founded in 1234, the present church was completed in 1311 and dissolved by Henry VIII in 1538. In the years that followed it was used as a guildhall, a hospital, a workhouse and a most dehumanising gaol. Today, it is the most complete example of Franciscan architecture in the country.

33 The north side of King Street, taken in 1866. King Street was created about a century earlier when the row of cottages that separated the street into Sun Lane and Back Lane was demolished by a draper named John Richards. He named it in honour of George III. Kings Road at this time linked into Duke Street, not King Street.

34 Looking towards the junction of West Street and Broad Street, where the *Vine Hotel* stood, *c*.1900. The picture captures the closing of the era of horse-drawn transport.

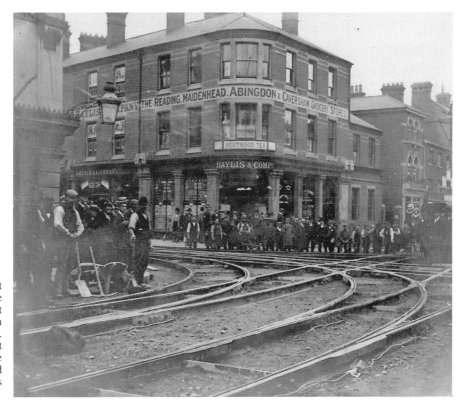

35 The St Mary's Butts/West Street/Broad Street junction. The local authority exercised its right to buy out the private tram company in 1901 for £13,000. They immediately brought forward plans to introduce electric trams. The complicated steelwork for the junction was specially made in America.

36 The northern terminus for the trams—Caversham Bridge, pictured *c*.1910. The old *Caversham Bridge Hotel* can be seen on the left. Earlier attempts to extend the trams into Caversham foundered when the Caversham Urban District Council refused to meet the cost of the road widening required at Berry's Corner.

37 & 38 *(below left and right)* Two views of Castle Street. The first is looking up the hill, roughly from the site of the present-day roundabout, *c*.1890. The *Horse and Jockey Inn*, on the opposite side of the road, has a history dating back to before 1699. The second picture shows Castle Street as a thriving shopping area in about 1910. Nobody now knows where Reading's castle stood, though Castle Hill seems a reasonable bet. It is thought the castle was destroyed by Henry II.

39 Poynder's bookshop, at the junction of Broad Street and Chain Street. Prior to about 1895, it had been the *Post Office Tavern* and today it is home to a men's outfitters.

40 Looking north along Duke Street from High Bridge, *c*.1910. The Duke in the name is probably Edward Seymour, the Duke of Somerset and uncle of the youthful King Edward VI. Among Seymour's other titles was Lord of Reading, and he was responsible for much of the destruction of Reading Abbey in the 1540s.

41 Looking north along the Caversham Road towards the *Caversham Bridge Hotel* in about 1905. Sheep appear to be wandering about in the middle of the road. As recently as the 1940s, animals were still being herded down Caversham Road to the market, but the days when sheep may safely graze in Caversham Road are now well and truly gone.

42 The view along Cross Street, looking towards Broad Street, in 1887. The area has a distinctly run-down look about it. On the earliest surviving map of Reading, it is referred to as 'Gutter Lane'.

43 Cemetery Junction in about 1903. The cemetery was founded by a private company in 1843, in response to chronic overcrowding in the town's churchyards. It lay outside the borough until 1887. Even in death, 'church' and 'chapel' were strictly segregated by the cemetery authorities.

44 Gun Street in 1908 looks relatively unchanged from the view you would see today.

Transport

Hone's General Coach Office
KING-STREET READING.
(Adjoining the George Inn,)

Reduced Fares to LONDON
BY THE
OMNIBUS.
Inside 8s. Outside 5s.

Mornings at 10 o'Clock.

TO LONDON
THE TELEGRAPH FAST COACH,

Through MAIDENHEAD and SLOUGH, every day at Twelve (except Sunday,) to *Nelson's* Black Bear, Piccadilly, and Blossom's Inn, Lawrence Lane, Cheapside; from whence it returns every Morning at 11; and Black Bear, Piccadilly at a quarter before 12.

———ooo———

"STAR" Coach to BATH and BRISTOL,

Through MARLBOROUGH, DEVIZES, and MELKSHAM, every Morning (except Sunday) at a quarter before Nine o'Clock to the York House Bath, and White Lion, BRISTOL.

TO LONDON.--The ZEPHYR, through WINDSOR,
Every day at half past One.

———ooo———

COACHES DAILY TO

Oxford	Brighton	Marlow	Portsmouth	Windsor
Wallingford	Guildford	Bath	Basingstoke	Wantage
Maidenhead	Petersfield	Bristol	Newbury	Faringdon
Winchester	Odiham	Horsham	Marlborough	Cirencester
Alton	Horndean	Southampton	Monmouth	Gloucester &
Farnham	Wycombe	Gosport	Hereford	Worthing.

Wm. HONE & Co. Proprietors.

	£	s.	d.
PAID OUT......			
CARRIAGE......			
BOOKING			
PORTERAGE....			

SOCIABLES to Streatley, Newbury, Basingstoke, Windsor, Wallingford, Henley and Maidenhead, daily

White, Printer & Binder, Reading.

45 An early 19th-century advertisement for Hones' Coaches of King Street. Queen Anne's trips to take the waters at Bath Spa made Reading a stop on a fashionable route. Although the coaching industry declined rapidly with the coming of the railways, a number of the town's 18th-century coaching inns remain.

46 The Great Western Railway came to Reading in 1840. This photograph shows the old down station in about 1850. Brunel built both the up and down stations on the south side of the railway, since virtually all of the town at that time lay to the south.

47 Despite its technical advantages, Brunel's broad gauge lost the battle to standardise the gauge on Britain's railways. Here, the last broad gauge train passes through Reading in May 1892.

48   The Imperial Tramways Company was licensed to run a tramway in the Borough in 1877. The first service went from Cemetery Junction to Brock Barracks on Oxford Road. This photograph shows one of the horsedrawn trams in Oxford Road, *c*.1890.

49 By the late 1930s, plans were being developed to replace the trams with trolley buses. As car number 7 waits at the Wokingham Road terminus, the newly-installed trolley bus wires signal the end of the days of the tram.

50 After the First World War, buses began to supplement the routes covered by the tramways. Here, we see two of the Corporation's first motor buses in Broad Street in about 1920.

51 Part of Reading's motor industry, the Speedwell Motor Company, occupied this Elizabethan building which stood at the junction of Broad Street and Minster Street. Queen Elizabeth I was said to have slept in the building, known in the 16th century as Walsingham House. It was demolished in 1905.

52 A more leisurely form of transport. Vincents of Castle Street built horsedrawn caravans. This is an example of their products from *c*.1900. A similar caravan can be seen in Blake's Lock Museum.

53 A 'Unic' taxicab on the forecourt of Hamilton Road Garage (Proprietor: L. Baker) which stood at the junction of Hamilton Road and Wokingham Road. The photograph dates from *c*.1927.

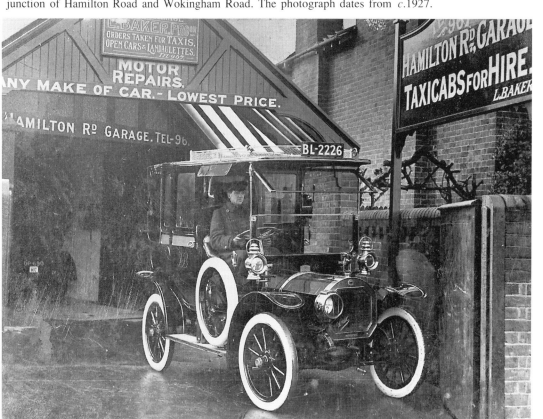

54 Steam power also played an important part in road transport. This picture shows a steam lorry dating from *c*.1900. It was owned by a firm of millers, Soundy and Company, who were based at Abbey Mill.

55 The Royal Balloon Aero Club fill up at Reading Gasworks in June 1906. At this time, before aircraft had proved themselves, balloons were important in both civil and military aviation, and had played a prominent part in the Boer War.

56 Reading had its own aircraft industry before the war. F.G. Miles, the aircraft designer, teamed up with Phillips and Powis at Woodley aerodrome in 1933. Their planes sold throughout the world and broke many records. Here, Mrs. Miles and their son look at one of the exhibits as Empire Air Day is celebrated at Woodley.

57 4 November 1938 ushered in a new era in public transport with the inauguration of an electric rail service between Reading and Waterloo.

Industry and Commerce

58 A delivery tricycle owned by Baylis and Company of 55-57 Erleigh Road. Tricycles like these, as well as conventional cycles, were made by the Warwick Company of Caversham Road, who exported their products around the world.

59   More deliveries—Tibble's Model Bakery of 76 Oxford Road posing for the camera in about 1930.

60   Heelas' premises at 22-27 Minster Street, *c*.1930. John Heelas started a draper's shop here in 1854. As his sons joined him in the business, he diversified into carpets, furniture and funeral direction. The family interest was bought out in 1947 by millionaire Charles Clore and in 1953 it became part of the John Lewis Group.

61 A shopping mall, 1906 style. Reading Arcade, built on the site of what is now Market Way. The Arcade, with its impressive colonnaded frontage to Broad Street, was one of Councillor J.C. Fidler's many contributions to the commercial heart of Reading. Others included Queen Victoria Street and part of West Street.

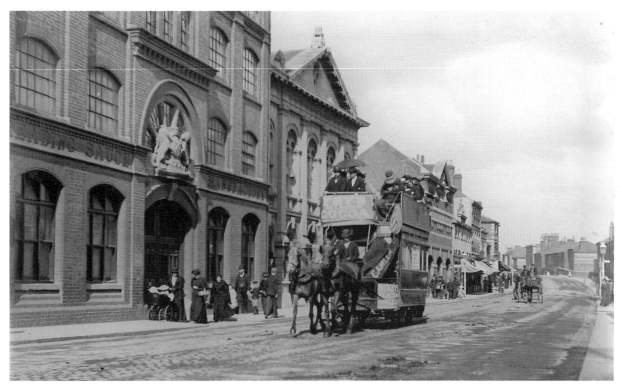

62 Cocks' Reading Sauce was once as famous as the Worcestershire variety. James Cocks set up as a fishmonger in Duke Street in 1789 and took up saucemaking in 1802. The product achieved national acclaim and even appears in Jules Verne's *Around the World in Eighty Days*. This shows his premises in Kings Road in about 1890, where the business survived until 1962.

63 The Reading Brush Factory stood next to St Giles' church on Southampton Street. This picture was taken in about 1908, but the firm survived here, later as a general hardware store, until the 1960s.

64 William McIlroy's department store on the Oxford Road, photographed shortly after its opening in 1903. The large expanse of glass at ground- and first-floor levels earned it the nickname of 'the crystal palace'. It closed as a department store in 1955.

65 The Kennet and Avon Canal was built to promote trade, and many industries grew up along its banks. This view, looking eastwards along Mill Lane in about 1895, captures two 19th-century landmarks. The water tower was built in the 1820s and, behind it, the mill has a history going back to Domesday Book.

66 Union Street, *c*.1908, a thriving retail street. 'Smelly Alley', as it is better known, has been assailing our nostrils since the 18th century with its variety of trades.

67 & **68** An undated picture of the Huntley and Palmer factory, showing part of their extensive private rail yards. Conventional locomotives could not operate inside the factory, so they used special 'fireless' locomotives which took their steam from a stationary boiler.

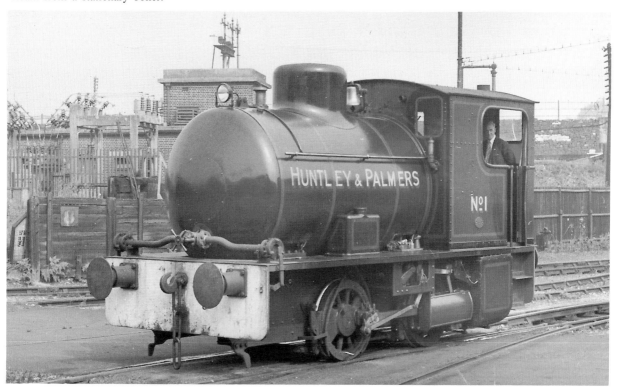

69 Proof of the worldwide reputation of Huntley and Palmer. Here Sir Ofori Atta KBE, Paramount Chief of Akim Akuakwa in the Gold Coast, visits the factory with his retinue. The year is 1928.

Seats of Learning

70 Reading University Extension College, seen from St Laurence's churchyard in about 1899. The new college extension can be seen to the rear. The college, opened in 1892, grew out of art and science classes, run under the auspices of the Department of Art and Science at South Kensington.

71 Celebrations in Valpy Street in 1898, as the University Extension College welcomes the Prince of Wales for the opening of its new building. The college started life in the old hospitium of Reading Abbey, shown on the preceding image.

72 The University College soon outgrew its premises in Valpy Street. A gift of £50,000 and land from Alfred Palmer, son of George Palmer, enabled it to move to a new site in London Road. Its old premises were occupied by the police station and magistrates' courts.

73 Part of the new college campus on London Road. The site included the Acacias, George Palmer's former home.

74 June 1905, and the Chancellor of Oxford University, Viscount Goschen, lays the foundation stone of the new University College buildings behind Portland Place.

75 Workmen building the Great Hall in 1906 pause for a photograph. It was opened later that year by Richard Haldene, the secretary of state for war.

76 The College became a university on 17 March 1926, but the acquisition of the Whiteknights estate, its current campus, was not completed until 1947. The name of Whiteknights comes from a white knight, Gilbert de Montalieu, son of a friend of William the Conqueror. His grave is said to lie near the Wokingham Road entrance to the estate. This picture shows the estate as it was in 1798, when it was acquired by the Marquis of Blandford.

77 'I have in my hand a piece of paper ...'. In 1938 Prime Minister Neville Chamberlain was made an honorary Doctor of Letters at the University. With him is the Chancellor, Sir Samuel Hoare.

Inns

78 The north side of Castle Street in about 1880. The *Sun Inn* was one of the coaching inns that flourished until the coming of the railways. St Mary's church at this time still had its unusual tower, 'The Pepper Box', which had to be removed for safety reasons in the 1950s.

79 The *Marquis of Granby* at Cemetery Junction, photographed in about 1906. It was originally called the *Gallows Tavern*, being the last place of refreshment for many prisoners en route to the nearby gallows. It was renamed after the Commander-in-Chief of the British army during the Seven Years' War, who owned the nearby Whiteknights estate.

80 You were rarely far from a pub in 19th-century Reading (except in Newtown where the Quaker Palmer family forbade their construction). This one picture of Southampton Street, taken in 1887, includes the *Reindeer Inn*, the *Little Crown Inn*, the *Lord Clyde Inn* and (for the teetotaller) the St Giles Coffee House.

81 The *Broad Face Inn* stood until 1926 on the site in the Market Place now occupied by Lloyds Bank. Samuel Pepys stayed there and the founder of the Society of Friends, George Fox, held some of his early meetings there. One explanation of the unusual name is that the inn sign shows the victim of a drowning or a hanging.

82 The *Three Tuns Inn* on Wokingham Road, seen in about 1890. From here, earlier in the century, Henry Addington and his home-made 'army', the Woodley Cavalry, planned how they would drive Napoleon's forces back into the sea, should they have had the temerity to invade.

83 The *Griffin Inn*, Church Road, Caversham, *c*.1890. Its demolition, some fifteen years later, can be seen in an earlier section of the book (see plate 18).

84 Not so much an inn as a hotel, and possibly the oldest railway hotel in the world, is the *Great Western Hotel* opposite the station. It dates from 1844 and it is thought Isambard Kingdom Brunel may have had a hand in its design. It closed as a hotel in 1972 and was converted into offices.

85 The *Merry Maidens* public house in Shinfield Road, photographed in about 1924. The statues of the maidens outside have since disappeared.

Reading Women

86 The Committee of the Women's Students Union at the University College, photographed with the Principal, Dr. W.M. Childs, in 1908. Almost half the people completing higher qualifications in the first year of the College were women. Childs went on to become the University's first Vice-Chancellor, from 1926 to 1929.

87 The women's suffrage movement began in the mid-19th century, but made slow progress until the more militant wing of the movement—the suffragettes—formed under the leadership of Mrs. Emmeline Pankhurst. This shows the premises of the Women's Social and Political Union in West Street, *c.*1911.

88 As the male working population were called to the Great War, it created opportunities for women. Here, 11 tram conductresses are recruited by Reading Corporation Tramways.

89 First World War newspaper propaganda. Mrs. Medland, wife of a blacksmith in the Oxford Road, turns her hand to making horse shoes for the British Army—'Doing our bit', as the sign behind them puts it.

90 The Second World War again gave women an opportunity to take over former male preserves. Here, women despatch riders take over from the men at southern region headquarters in Reading, in 1941.

Occasions

91 The Palmer family made many contributions to the life of Reading. They endowed the University College, helped to fund the new town hall and museum, donated King's Meadow as a public recreation ground and, in 1891, provided and laid out the 49 acres of Palmer Park. This picture was taken at its opening. Note the penny farthing bicycles in the foreground.

92   There is nothing on the photograph to say so, but the gathered crowds suggest that this may be the opening of the Caversham Free Library in 1907. The library was endowed by the Scottish-born philanthropist Andrew Carnegie. The site was formerly occupied by the playground to Caversham House Academy.

93   Reading's Cooperative movement was founded in 1860 by Stephen Gyngell, a 28-year-old apprentice at Reading Ironworks. But it was not until September 1928 that they opened their present store on Cheapside. The Mayor, John Rabson (after whom the recreation ground was named), performed the opening ceremony.

94 & 95 Great excitement greeted the opening of the electric tram service. The crowds packed Broad Street, Oxford Road and Mill Lane on 22 July 1903 to watch the celebrations. Unseemly scenes took place as crowds struggled to board the first trams. New routes were introduced between Whitley and Caversham bridge, and from Erleigh Road and Bath Road.

96 19 February 1912 and Prospect Street, Caversham is brought to a halt by the funeral of William Trobe. He was a military man, a veteran of Crimea and the Indian Mutiny of 1857-8, who lived in Westfield Road. The band of his old regiment, the 2nd Yorkshires, turned out to lead the cortège.

97 Crowds gather in Market Place during the General Strike of 1926 to listen to a speaker.

98 Broad Street, seen from the top of a tram in 1937. The decorations are for the impending Coronation of King George VI. The imposing entrance to the Reading Arcade can be seen on the extreme right of the picture.

99 The crowds gathered again to see the last tram run, on 20 May 1939. Over the years, the trams carried 155 million passengers and travelled 12.5 million miles. The crowd sang Auld lang syne as the Mayor took the controls on the journey from Broad Street to the depot.

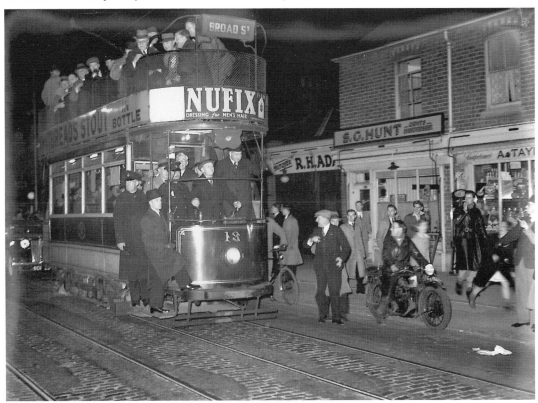

100 Private Frank Golder was repatriated to his home in Vachel Road in November 1943 after three and a half years in a prisoner of war camp. He found the street decorated to welcome him back and the crowds around the car were so dense that he had to walk the last part of the way home, on a wooden leg that he had made for himself during his imprisonment.

Disasters

101 The inner gateway of Reading Abbey, at the time of its collapse in 1861. Its restoration was overseen by Giles Gilbert Scott, an architect whose other works include the Home Office, the Albert Memorial and Reading prison.

102 At 12.30 a.m. on 23 July 1904, a fire broke out at Serpell's biscuit factory in South Street. It was through the roof before the fire brigade were called, and once they arrived they were hampered by a severe water shortage. The building was totally destroyed and damage was estimated at £30,000.

103 Crowds gather to watch the Caversham fire brigade's vain attempts to save the cottages on Prospect Street, next to the *Prince of Wales* public house, in 1907. In the 1840s, one of the cottages had served as the local school.

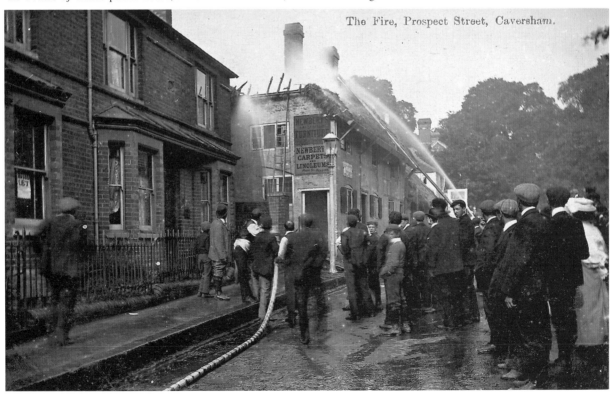

104 In June 1910, three days of freak storms left the Oxford Road area under water. Here, the Fire Brigade struggle to answer an emergency call further along the Oxford Road. When they arrived, the floods had put out the fire in the engine's steam pump!

105 Great Knollys Street has suffered from repeated flooding over the years, including this one in December 1929. The street takes its name from the family who owned the land on which it was built. Sir Francis Knollys was an adventurer who was married to a cousin of Queen Elizabeth I.

106 The great house at Caversham Park was acquired by the Catholic Oratory school in 1922, and was their home until 1943, when the BBC Monitoring Service took it over. On 30 August 1926 the school suffered a serious fire. It also led to a controversy about Reading's fire appliances being called to deal with fires outside the borough boundary (as Caversham Park then was).

107 S. and E. Collier were the best known of Reading's brickworks, supplying the raw materials for many well-known buildings around the country. In August 1938 a serious fire broke out at their premises at Water Road, Tilehurst. Here, the fire brigade struggle to keep the blaze under control. The firm survived and continued trading until 1965.

108 The floods in the winter of 1947 were the worst this century, adding to the misery of post-war austerity. Some 1,600 houses were flooded, some up to three feet deep. Essential services were cut off and there were even shortages of drinking water. Nevertheless, the people of Caversham tried to maintain some semblance of normal life.

Rich and Poor

109 *(above)* Silver Street was for a long time one of the poorest parts of the town and contained some of the worst slum housing. It was said that hordes of rats ran out from some of them as they were demolished. The cottages here were demolished in around 1927, shortly after this photograph was taken. The street's name derives from Seivier Street—where sieves were once made.

110 *(above right)* A survey in 1912 showed that one in five of Reading families were living in serious poverty, unable to maintain even the most basic standards of health. These children may have been residents of Silver Street—the photographer, Mr. May, was based in nearby London Street.

111 *(right)* The Government promised soldiers returning from the Great War 'Homes fit for heroes'. In Reading, the promise began to be carried out by the provision of a council housing estate on the Shinfield Road, seen here under construction in 1924.

112 The Vachell family owned the Coley estate from the 14th to the 18th centuries. Thomas Vachell was the town's Member of Parliament at the time Henry VIII dissolved the monasteries. In 1634 they endowed these almshouses on Castle Street, photographed here in about 1890.

113 At the other end of the social scale was Caversham Park. For many years, it was the home of the Crawshay family—the ironfounders who established the great ironworks at Merthyr Tydfil.

Caversham Park & Lake, 654.

Rivers and Canals

114 Caversham bridge as it was before 1869. The Reading end of the bridge was once a drawbridge, pulled up for defensive purposes during the Civil War siege. Because neither the authorities in Reading nor those in Caversham would take responsibility for its upkeep, the bridge spent much of its 750 years in a ruinous state.

115 Chestnut Walk (called Abbot's Walk on this picture), the attractive canalside walk by the Abbey ruins and the prison. This picture shows the castle-like design of the prison before its remodelling in 1971.

116 The 'half and half' Caversham bridge was replaced in 1869 by this iron structure. Its appearance was widely condemned and it soon proved to be too narrow for the volume of traffic wanting to use it. It was in its turn replaced by the present bridge, which was opened by the Prince of Wales in 1926.

117 The steam launch *Eclipse*, pictured at Caversham bridge. The house in the picture, named Piper's Cottage after a local ferryman, was actually moved—in one piece—by about eight feet during the construction of the iron bridge.

118 A steam boat enters Caversham lock in 1912. The first steam boat to be seen on the Thames in Reading was in 1813 and they were commonplace from the 1860s onwards. A thriving boatbuilding industry lined the banks of the Thames in Reading in the late 19th and early 20th centuries.

Reading at Play

119 *(left)* The Borough Council acquired the Thameside Promenade in 1907 and laid it out as a recreational area. This was threatened for a time by Bradfield Rural District Council's plans to build a sewage works at Scours Lane, just upwind of it! This picture dates from *c*.1920. Note the First World War tank on display on the left of the picture.

120 *(below left)* The gentlemen of the Reading Natural History Association, suitably attired for an outing to Bucklebury on 1 August 1881.

121 *(below)* Leisurely Edwardian days in the Forbury Gardens. Some special event seems to be going on, for it looks as if a marquee has been erected just off the picture, to the left.

122 The Palace Theatre in Cheapside was founded by local businessmen in 1907, and was built in the grandest of Edwardian luxury. It survived until after the Second World War, when competition from the cinemas and television gradually forced it out of business. It was redeveloped for offices in 1961.

123 Three cinemas opened in Reading in 1909. The most successful of these was the Vaudeville Electric Theatre, which stood on the north side of Broad Street, opposite Chain Street. It was rebuilt in 1921 in a style that earned it the title 'Reading's temple of colour and harmony'.

124 Huntley and Palmer staff in three horsedrawn wagonettes, about to go on an excursion. The picture was taken in Gosbrook Road, Caversham in about 1914.

READING FOOTBALL CLUB LTD., 1906-7

H. J. Matthews, A. Weir, E. Gettins, W. Whittaker, J. Comrie, C. Brown, J. R. Blandford, R. Lloyd
(Secretary.) (Directors.)

H. Smith, J. Warburton, A. Turnbull, W. Godley, W. Mc Cafferty, M. Allman, H. Grundy, F. Paley,
(Director.) W. Hart. A Lindsay, (Trainer.)

Photo by W. H. Dee, Huntley Studio. Reading.

125 Reading Football Club's first team in the 1906/7 season. It was not one of their most auspicious seasons. They finished towards the bottom of the Southern League and gate receipts fell so much that the *Berkshire Chronicle* had to organise a sixpenny fund appeal to pay the team's wages during the close season.

126 The hunt prepares to move out from the *Roebuck Inn*, in Tilehurst. Other venues for hunts shown in old photographs included the *Grenadier* pub at Basingstoke Road, Whitley and, on one occasion, the town hall.

The Great War

127 The people of Reading read the proclamation of mobilisation, posted outside the town hall in August 1914.

128 *(right)* Lords Curzon and Reading lead a recruitment drive for the armed forces in September 1914. Lord Reading was the noted barrister Rufus Isaacs, who served as Lord Chief Justice, Ambassador to the United States of America, Viceroy of India, Foreign Secretary—and Member of Parliament for Reading.

129 *(below)* Soldiers parade in Friar Street during the early days of the war.

130 *(below right)* Pupils of the George Palmer School are pressed into the war effort. They are making wooden hospital appliances for the Reading War Hospital Supplies Department. Education was severely disrupted by the war, with schools being commandeered as hospitals, barracks and refugee centres. Many pupils were forced to go onto half-time education.

131 A poignant picture of the 35th Divisional Company, Royal Engineers, leaving Reading station for training in Ripon on 16 July 1915. By January next year, they would be in the trenches of France, taking part in the battles of the Somme and Passchendaele.

132 Market Place on 27 November 1917. The Distinguished Conduct Medal is presented to Sergeant W.H. Ridley of the Royal Garrison Artillery, one of several soldiers to be decorated at the ceremony.

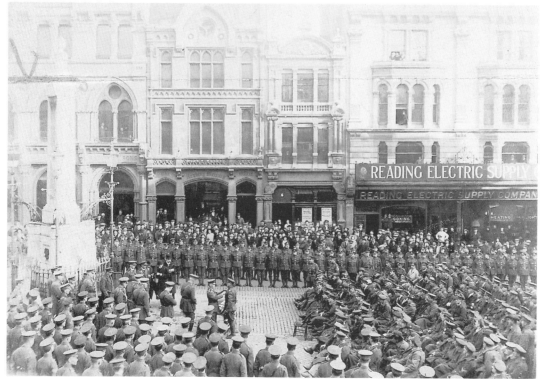

133 Part of the parade along Friar Street to mark the end of hostilities in 1918.

Peace Celebrations Reading

1930s Reading

134 & 135 Two views of pre-war schooldays. In the first, the children of the Oxford Road Primary School celebrate Empire Day with a tableau of St George and the dragon. In the second, children at the Hemdean Road Council School (now Caversham Primary School) learn about road safety at pedestrian crossings with the aid of tricycles and dolls' prams.

136 New Town, seen from the Kennet and Avon Canal in 1938, before the extensive redevelopment. It was in the news that year because of council plans to install safety railings along the water's edge.

137 As traffic grew, new measures had to be brought in to control it. Here, drivers struggle to master the complexities of new arrangements for traffic circulation outside the station. Note the capacious pram on the pavement to the right of the picture.

138 Jack Hobbs was one of England's greatest batsmen, playing for his country from 1907 to 1930. Here, he passes on some hints to admiring pupils from Reading School. He was there for a match between the school and a Mr. Kempton's eleven in 1938.

139 August 1939, and the crowds at Emmer Green Fête are entertained by a vaulting display from Major Ellershaw's Happy Elves.

Reading at War: 1939-45

140-143 Four interesting things to do in a gas mask. In the first, a decontamination squad give a display of anti-gas measures in the Corporation yard. Staff at Huntley and Palmer try out the latest fashion accessory. Great Western Railway staff display what looks to me like a distinct lack of respect for an incendiary bomb, as they are taught how to put them out. Finally, cyclists from the Palmer Park Cycle Racing League come up with an idea that could have applications in today's pollution-laden traffic jams.

144 The finishing touches are put to the air raid shelter in Market Place. Shelters were constructed throughout the town centre but, happily, the town only suffered one serious raid during the course of the war. Forty-one people were killed when a single bomber destroyed the area around the People's Pantry, a restaurant at the Friar Street end of the Market Arcade.

145 Other air raids on the town had less serious consequences than the one that destroyed the People's Pantry. This bomb left a large crater in a field in Whitley. The police are looking into it.

146 Wartime petrol shortages affected life in all sorts of ways. The Huntley and Palmer sales force abandoned their cars for bicycles and, here, one of Reading's Comficabs has been converted to run on gas. The date is November 1939.

147 & 148 Queueing for everything became a way of life for Reading people during the war. In these pictures, women queue outside the town hall to register for fire watching and a serpentine queue winds its way around Market Place in May 1941 in response to a rumour that 5,000 oranges were coming up for sale.

149 Battle rages in the streets of Tilehurst in 1942. It is part of a Home Guard exercise, clearly providing a good deal of entertainment for the onlooking residents.

150 Wings for Victory week, in which the people of Reading were encouraged to contribute towards the war effort in the air. Part of the event was a parade past the town hall. The boarded-up window of the church and the damaged buildings across the road are a reminder of the recent air raid.

151 'Next year we'll save up for the rest of the plane!'. The Mayor tries out a link trainer, part of a Wings for Victory display at the town hall. With him is the Minister of Fuel and Power, Major Gwilym Lloyd-George.

152 June 1944 and Joe Louis, the world heavyweight champion boxer (and serving in the U.S. forces) fights Elza 'Tommy' Thompson at Elm Park football ground. The local press, taking security somewhat to excess, refer to the fight taking place 'at a stadium in the home counties'.

153 *(above left)* The people of Reading celebrate victory in 1945. The formal celebrations took the time-honoured form of a parade past the town hall. The buildings damaged in the bombing raid in 1943 had by then been demolished.

154 *(below left)* Many communities in Reading celebrated victory in the war with a street party. This one was in De Beauvoir Road.

155 *(above)* Reading Thanksgiving week, in October 1945. It was opened by a parade and here in the Forbury instruments of war become playthings for excited children.

Caversham

156 St Peter's church, Caversham, suffered serious damage during the Civil War battle for the control of Caversham Bridge in 1643. Its tower was replaced by a wooden structure which lasted until the church's restoration in 1878/9. This early photograph shows the church before its restoration.

157 Prospect Street, at the junction of the Peppard and Henley roads, c.1880. The cottages on the left, on the site now occupied by the pub car park, were destroyed by a fire in 1907. The fire can be seen in plate 103.

158 Bridge Street, Caversham, decorated for Queen Victoria's golden jubilee in 1887.

159 The view from Caversham Bridge, *c*.1890. The eel traps or bucks can be seen in the river. On the right bank are St Peter's church and the grounds of Caversham Court. The grounds remain as a public garden, though the house itself was demolished in 1933.

160 The smithy stood near Berry's Corner and was photographed in the 1890s. The proprietor, Mr. Eynott, is seen between two helpers. In his spare time, Mr. Eynott was a member of the Caversham handbell-ringing team.

161 F.G. Horne, stonemason, had his premises on Church Road. This picture dates from *c*.1905.

162 Church Street, Caversham, looking eastwards in about 1900. Caversham House School is on the right of the picture and Holt & Co., drapers can be seen in the distance.

163 Church Street, Caversham again, now looking westwards, *c*.1910. The drapery shown in the previous picture has now changed hands to become Cox and Co. Harry Eynott, fruiterer, shown on the right, is presumably a relative of the blacksmith in plate 160.

164 & 165 Public services in Caversham, just prior to its absorption into Reading in 1911. The Caversham Urban District Council fire brigade, *c*.1910; and a horse bus outside the *Prince of Wales* public house in Prospect Street, photographed at the turn of the century.

166 Baylis and Company, grocers of Church Road, celebrate the coronation of King George V in June 1911. Mr. James and Mr. Wiggins, the deliverymen, pose with the shop staff. Next door are the premises of Green's, the photographers. The founder, Joseph Green, was an upholsterer and coffin maker.

167 A reminder of the more rural nature of parts of Caversham at the turn of the century. The Warren was at this time more like a country lane. Its name comes from the nearby rabbit warren, which was farmed for its meat by the Mapledurham Estate.

168 The junction of Peppard Road and Kidmore End Road, in what looks to be the mid-1930s. The *White Horse* is still part of the Simonds brewing empire. The dragon over Hodge's post office stores was originally over the blacksmith's shop that stood on the same site. It was made in Emmer Green brickworks.

169 This photograph was taken roughly from the point where St Barnabas Road joins Surley Row. The imposing building on the right is Grove Farm, a 16th-century building which survives to this day—now known as Old Grove House.

170 St Barnabas' church, Emmer Green, photographed *c.*1907. The present church was not built until 1924 and, at this time, the meeting hall to the rear provided a place of worship. There also appears to have been a pond on the opposite side of Grove Road.

Tilehurst

Prospect Park,
Reading.

171 Prospect Park was acquired by the Council in 1901 for the use of Reading people. The acquisition was largely due to the far-sightedness of Councillor J.C. Fidler, who lived at one time at Prospect Hill House, the mansion in the park.

172 The railway came through Tilehurst in 1840, but it was not until 1882 that a station was built to serve the growing population.

173 Mr. A. Ilsley, the proprietor of the Tilehurst omnibus, pictured in about 1900. This, and carriers' carts, were the main public transport until 1919, when motor bus services began running from the *Plough Inn*.

174 Church Road, Tilehurst (known today as St Michael's Road) runs between School Road and St Michael's church, past Churchend Copse. For the children of 1911, being in a photograph has much the same fascination as would appearing on television for a modern child.

175 St Michael's church was founded in 1189 or earlier, though the present structure dates from the late 13th or early 14th century and the tower is 18th century. This photograph is undated, but the church looks much as it did at the turn of the century.

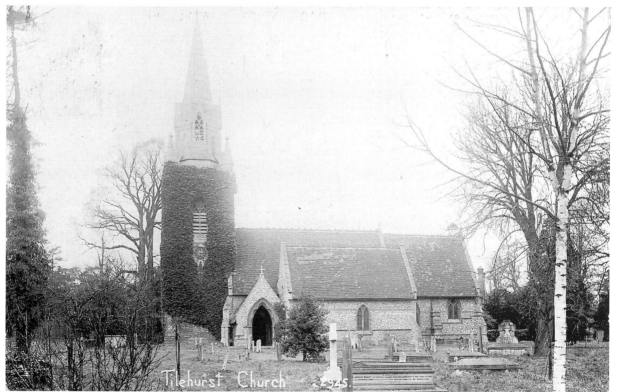

A.252.

176 Tilehurst begins to grow. This picture shows Kentwood Hill in the early years of its development. Kentwood (or Kenetwode as it was spelt in the 12th century) was an area of woodland stretching from the Thames to the Kennet. A Nicholas Kentwood was listed as a parishioner of Tilehurst church in 1341.

Kentwood Hill, Tilehurst. 2947.

School Road Tilehurst

177 & 178   School Road and School End, Tilehurst. Tilehurst's first school was built at School Road in 1819. The National School, as it was called, was built by the National Society for Promoting the Education of the Poor in the Principles of the Established Church, on land given by the Rector of Tilehurst.

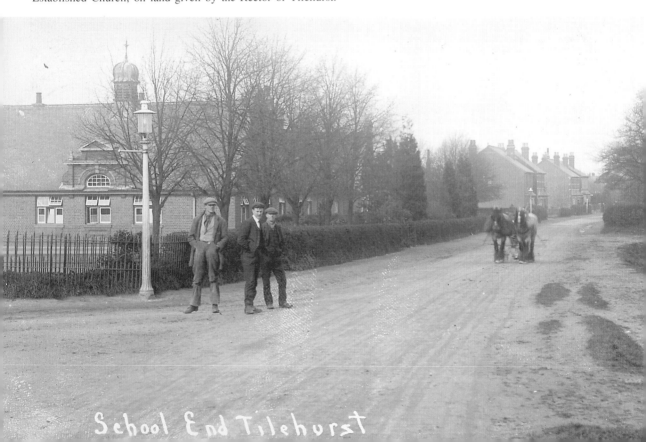

School End Tilehurst

179   The *Roebuck* was built in the 1880s to cater for boating parties and anglers. The Great Western Railway tried to close the footbridge shown in the picture in 1897. An outraged Parish Council produced four ancient local residents, who testified that there had been a right of way across there before the days of the railway.

Select Bibliography

I have listed below a number of books for the reader who wants to learn more of the town's history. You will find them and many others in the local history section of Reading Central Library.

Alexander, Alan, *Borough Government and Politics: Reading 1835-1985*, Allen & Unwin, 1985.
Babbage, Terry, *Tylehurst Described—An Historical Account*, Berkshire County Council.
Hylton, Stuart, *Reading Places, Reading People*, Berkshire Books, 1992.
Kift, Mary, *Life in Old Caversham*, published privately, 1980.
Phillips, Daphne, *The Story of Reading*, Countryside Books, 1980.
Southerton, P.G., *Reading in Old Photographs*, Alan Sutton, 1988.

Norman arch